CW00504134

BITCOIN

FOR BEGINNERS

The complete guide on how bitcoin blockchain work to earn money.

BY LUKE CLARK

INTRODUCTION: 6

BITCOIN CHAPTER 1 THE FUTURE OF BITCOIN 7

THE TECHNICAL HURDLES 8
THE FUNDAMENTAL HURDLES 9
LOOKING OR SOLUTIONS 10
UTILIZING BITCOINS FOR INTERNATIONAL TRAVEL 11
LESS EXORBITANT 11
ALL-INCLUSIVE 11
SECURE 11
HELPFUL 12
IRREVERSIBLE 12
THE BEST BITCOIN TRADING PLATFORMS 12
CEX.IO: 12
BITSTAMP: 13
COINBASE: 13
BITFINEX: 14
KRAKEN: 14
IS BITCOIN GATHERING OVER? 15
ADVANCED CURRENCY 16
BITCOINS & NEW AMAZON COIN TAKING OVER THE WORLD 19
ARE AMAZON COINS A VIRTUAL CURRENCY LIKE BITCOIN? 19
IT'S ALL ABOUT THE APP 20
EXCHANGE BITCOINS AND GET THE MOST OUT OF IT 21
BITCOIN BROKERS AND THE GROWING POPULARITY OF BITCOINS 22
GUIDELINE 22
IN CASE OF MISFORTUNE 23
TURNING INTO A SIGNIFICANT INSTALLMENT SYSTEM 23
BITCOINS AND CRIMINAL OPERATIONS 23
BITCOIN CAN MAKE ASSET MANAGERS OF US ALL – HOW? 24
HOW BITCOIN WILL PROMOTE LATIN AMERICAN GROWTH? 25
BITCOIN'S IMPACT ON STATE-ARRANGED ECONOMIES 25
BITCOIN'S SPECIFIC ROLE IN THE ECONOMIC GROWTH OF THE PACIFIC COUNTRIES 26

BITCOIN CHAPTER 2 – BITCOIN MARKETPLACE 28

ABOUT BITCOIN 28
HOW DOES BITCOIN WORK? 29
HOW DID BITCOIN START? 29
HOW WOULD I CONTRIBUTE? 30
HOW IS BITCOIN MADE? 30
PURCHASE AND HOLD 30
BITCOIN AS SHARES 31
EXCHANGING BITCOIN 31
WHY TO PUT RESOURCES INTO BITCOIN? 32
FOR WHAT REASON DO I REQUIRE BITCOIN NEWS? 33

ADVANTAGE AND DISADVANTAGES OF BITCOIN 33
THE TRUE STORY OF THE BITCOIN MARKET AND ITS PHENOMENAL COURSE 37
CORRELATION BETWEEN GOLD AND BITCOIN 39
NO SWELLING 41
CONVENIENCE 42
DIMINISHED EXTORTION 42
FEWER CHARGES AND FAST EXCHANGES 42
STEPS TO GET $10 OF FREE BITCOIN, EASY AND SIMPLE 44
HOW TO BUY BITCOINS? 45
HOW THEN CAN ONE BUY BITCOINS? 45

BITCOIN CHAPTER 3 ALL ABOUT BITCOIN CRYPTOCURRENCY 46

ABOUT BITCOIN CRYPTOCURRENCY 47
KEY TERMS RELATED TO BITCOIN CRYPTOCURRENCY 47
THINGS YOU CAN DO WITH BITCOIN 48
WHAT IS A CRYPTOCURRENCY? 48
WHAT IS THE BENEFIT? 49
WHAT IS THE BEGINNING OF BITCOIN? 49
SO, WHAT IS BITCOIN? 50
FOR WHAT REASON DO PEOPLE CARE ABOUT BITCOIN? 50
COINBASE AND BITCOIN STARTUP 52
CONTEST IS COMING 53
ADMINISTRATIVE SECURITY REMAINS INTENSE 54
WALL STREET CHANGES FROM BASHING BIT TO CRYPTOCURRENCY BACKER - HOW 54
WHY USE BITCOIN? 55
SAFER THAN BANKS 55
LOWER ADMINISTRATION EXPENSES THAN BANKS 55
OKAY OF BREAKDOWN 56
OKAY OF SWELLING 56
THE FAR-REACHING IMPLICATIONS OF THE BITCOIN PROTOCOL 56
SIMPLE 3-STEP GUIDE TO BUYING YOUR FIRST BITCOIN 58
WHY SO POPULAR? 59
SO HERE ARE 3 SIMPLE STRIDES TO PURCHASING BITCOINS: 59
CHOOSE WHERE TO BUY 60
ODDS OF USING BITCOINS FOR ILLEGAL ACTIVITIES 60
ODDS OF EMPLOYMENTS FOR CRIMINAL OPERATIONS 61
BITCOINS AND TAXES 61
GUIDELINE OF THE FRAMEWORK 61
5 TIPS TO CONSIDER BEFORE INVESTING IN BITCOIN 62
BECOME FAMILIAR WITH THE BASICS FIRST 62
SET CLEAR TARGETS 62
PUT RESOURCES INTO BITCOIN 63
CONSIDER THE MARKET CAP 63
ENHANCE YOUR INVESTMENTS 63
SHREWD BITCOIN STRATEGIES TO ACCUMULATE GOLD BULLION 63

DISCOVER AN ORGANIZATION THAT SELLS GOLD BULLION 63
BEGIN MINING BITCOIN ONLINE OR OFFLINE 63
OPEN AN ONLINE BITCOIN WALLET 64
BUY GOLD BULLION WITH BITCOIN 64
WHAT MAKES BITCOIN DIFFERENT? 64

CONCLUSION: **66**

Introduction:

Seemingly perhaps the most problematic, energizing, and disputable new improvements in worldwide financial matters, the appearance of bitcoin as a genuine, well-known currency has started inciting extreme discussion concerning the "future" of the world economy.

That being said, numerous people haven't been familiar with this new, online-just monetary asset, to a great extent because of its prohibition from the "genuine" world. The beginnings of bitcoin can be followed back to 2008, when 'Satoshi Nakamoto', an alias by the maker of the currency, acquainted his 'peer-with peer' money to the world.

Bitcoin is characterized as a 'digital currency,' or type of currency that is produced and moved to utilize a variety of cryptographic devices rather than focal government specialists. The bitcoin is intended to stay 'free' from public interests and collaborations, creating 'worth' out of its power and protection from expansion. Bitcoins are a virtual item that has numerous comparative properties to customary money. Using solid cryptography and a shared organization, they fill in as the main money without a focal backer. Bitcoins are not actual elements but rather work in essentially a similar manner.

For those keen on utilizing bitcoin as a vehicle for unfamiliar trade, an assortment of stages as of now exist which consider intra-currency exchanging. A portion of the bigger stages are Kraken, VirWox, Mt. Gox, and Intersango. Every one of these trade vehicles includes a remarkable arrangement of services and specifications.

Security assumes an extraordinarily significant part in bitcoin exchanging because of both the elusive idea of currency and the absence of an extensive administrative system for the trades. That being said, these money trade programming stages draw in innumerable guests, by far most of whom can take part in exchanges without inconvenience.

The worth of bitcoin is normally unpredictable, to a great extent because of the way that currency is a mainstream device for people trading illicit services who wish to stay unknown. Late government-upheld captures of bitcoin have made the worth of the money vacillate enormously. That being said, the per-unit worth of bitcoin has risen cosmically in recent years. For those keen on becoming familiar with bitcoins, an assortment of online assets and money trade programming bundles give data in regards to the essentials.

Bitcoin Chapter 1 The Future of Bitcoin

Bitcoin - At the Crossroads of the Future

As people everywhere in the world increment their awareness about the digital money insurgency, venture specialists are arranging to state their viewpoints. Lately, the supporters of crypto forecasters are anticipating numbers that challenge gravity. The numbers are stunning. On the opposite side of the fence, we discover the doubters. There is a lot of all-around regarded monetary expert who isn't reluctant to caution people about the venture bubble.

Some even concede that cryptographic forms of money may in any case have some play left in them, however sometimes, the air pocket will explode, and people will get injured. To commute home their point, they just need to ponder the IPO air pocket of 2001.

The Technical Hurdles

The cryptographic money upset is as yet in its early stages. In that capacity, most coins, Bitcoin notwithstanding, are exchanging without verifiable markers to help financial backers. It is an unrestricted economy in the most perfect structure. Sadly, unregulated economy exchanging is defenseless to impact from all headings. Thusly the main problem is brought to light for cryptographic money financial backers. With no set of experiences to count on, financial backers need to settle on choices dependent on their gut.

The impediments that confound the dynamic cycle for Bitcoin financial backers are bounty. The coin is consistently helpless to the specialized parts of exchanging. The dramatic expansion in cost is being driven by appeal and scant items. However, financial backers get a little fidgety when the cost increments to an extreme, excessively quick. Then, we see the normal rectification that comes when a venture becomes overbought. The issue is these revisions are ending up being brutal, which tests the determination of financial backers who aren't utilized to such undeniable degrees of unpredictability.

Saving specialized investigation, technology issues are additionally driving the market today. There's no rejecting that the cryptographic money market has had its issues. After announcing blockchain technology to be the securest way to deal with scattering data, some openings are being uncovered practically day by day. The bugs will get worked out as this sort of technology appears to be bound for the ideal time. Tragically, Bitcoin has blockchain technology under a magnifying lens at this moment.

Regardless of how secure any system may profess to be, programmers make certain to uncover the shortcomings in a rush. The digital currency industry has effectively been assaulted by programmers, who have taken billions of dollars in Bitcoin and other crypto coins. Losing currency to programmers will in general make financial backers somewhat jumpy. It likewise makes for a lot of cases from those hurt by technology that may not yet be a safe as guaranteed.

The Fundamental Hurdles

There's a familiar proverb: When teachers and janitors begin making millions from contributing, costs will crash since we need teachers and janitors. Governments get apprehensive when their occupants begin losing currency or raking in tons of currency without making good on charges. It's no fortuitous event that India and South Korea are among the most dynamic nations on the cryptographic money trades, yet the two governments are thinking about restricting the exchanging of all cryptos. The US, conceivably the world's greatest Bitcoin player, is working in Congress to conclude how to direct the cryptographic money market.

They have effectively restricted a few trades for conceivable false movement. China is examining an inside and out boycott while Europe appears to be ready to take cues from America. If Bitcoin or some other cryptographic money tries to turn into a worldwide currency for regular installments, achievement would be predicated on the world's greatest economies participating in the procession. Shockingly, the significant players (referenced above) appear to be moving the other way.

The greatest concern is by all accounts Bitcoin's appeal to the criminal component. Evidence has been introduced that shows North Korea has been taking Bitcoin to help account for its atomic program. ISIS regularly moves currency among its subsidiaries using Bitcoin, doing so undetected until it's past the point of no return. The medication exchange is additionally appreciating the secrecy managed the cost of them by blockchain technology.

Looking or Solutions

Generally, people are keen on all parts of cryptographic money. Bitcoin has effectively shown the potential for effectively settling installment issues among clients and sellers. However, trust is a major issue going ahead. If the obscurity highlight is the main thrust behind the digital currency insurgency, it will be difficult to get governments to move onboard and endorse crypto-exchanging.

We should take a gander at how South Korea chose to determine the Bitcoin issue. The South Korean government as of late passed a bill that gives six Korean banks a position to allow its client to exchange Bitcoin from their ledgers. There's only one specification: the record must be opened in the client's genuine name. Poof. There goes the secrecy include. However, South Koreans can in any case exchange Bitcoin through a Bitcoin Wallet insofar as tax avoidance isn't the explanation they need to do as such. It's a decent trade-off, yet its allure might be restricted.

Throughout the following not many months, financial backers should begin finding solutions to a ton of inquiries. Until that time, the estimating of Bitcoin and other cryptographic forms of money will stay unstable. The cost will expand given interest yet will drop each time another issue becomes news. Until costs balance out, people should focus on one principle of contributing. Never put away more currency than you can bear to lose. Bitcoin is arriving at its junction.

In our current reality where accommodation is put at a higher cost than normal, the vast majority need to manage something convenient and stay away from an excess of problem. Being virtual money, bitcoins have progressively begun supplanting the cumbersome conventional banknotes and checks.

Organizations and banks are directing awareness lobbies for their clients to take up this method of installment, as it is tranquil and efficient. The fundamental benefit is that you can follow past exchanges and trade rates on a Bitcoin Chart. Below are some reasons why you should place bitcoins in your list of entire necessities:

Less exorbitant

When you exchange utilizing currency, you are dependent upon unexpected value changes in fundamental items. You wind up spending substantially more than you had planned given correctional trade rates. Bitcoins are the worldwide currency that has stable rates and esteem and will save you time and high charges.

All-inclusive

When you are voyaging, the way toward trading money is very lumbering. Moreover, conveying a lot of money isn't tedious yet in addition unsafe. Bitcoins give you the solace of conveying as much currency as you need in a virtual state. It is regular among brokers everywhere in the world and thus saves you the bother of managing more than one currency.

Secure

Bitcoins are extortion evidence because of the weighty cryptography that goes into their making. There are no rates of hacking or spilling of people's very own data. When you utilize the ordinary currency move techniques abroad, you are probably going to fall under the control of programmers who may invade your financial balances. With bitcoins, you alone approach your record and can approve any currency into and from it.

Helpful

Dissimilar to typical banks that require evidence of ID to open a record, bitcoins permit anybody to get to it without requesting verification. Exchanges are moment and are not restricted by geological limits or time regions, and there is no desk work included. To join bitcoins, you just need to download the bitcoin wallet and make a record.

Irreversible

Bitcoins shield you from such occurrences, as these exchanges can't be switched. You ought to be cautious with your bitcoins to try not to move them to some unacceptable person.

The Best Bitcoin Trading Platforms

The digital currency has not just given the quickest method to move currency yet, in addition, another element to exchange with and to bring in currency separated from the stocks and different wares. There are a lot of trades where exchanging Bitcoin is protected and gotten and the clients are worked with many broadened services.

Being a digital money financial backer or merchant you can pick any of the trades for your solace. The following is a short survey of top Bitcoin trades throughout the planet.

CEX.IO:

One of the most established and rumored trades which was begun in 2013, London a Bitcoin Trading trade and as a cloud mining facilitator. Later its mining power developed tremendously that it held almost 50% of the organization's mining limits; nonetheless, it has been presently shut.

"CEX.IO" permits clients to extend to a lot bigger measure of Bitcoin exchanges, and it has the office to make accessible the

Bitcoin at the mentioned cost in a split second. However, this trade charges a somewhat high trade sum, yet this is made up for the security and offices of permitting multi-currency exchanges (Dollar, Euro, and Ruble) to purchase Bitcoin.

Bitstamp:

It was established in 2011 and is the most seasoned of trades that offer digital money and Bitcoin exchanges. The most regarded because despite being the most seasoned it has never been under security danger and tills as of late. Bitstamp as of now upholds four monetary standards Bitcoin, Ethereum, Litecoin, and Ripple, and is accessible with the versatile application also, aside from site to exchange.

It has flawless help for the European clients or the dealers having their records in Euro Banks. The security is progressed and of cold stockpiling type, which implies the coins are put away disconnected. So you can say it is completely unrealistic for any programmer to invade. Finally, its unpredictable UI recommends that it isn't for the amateur client yet for experts and it offers generally low exchange charges.

CoinBase:

It is presumably perhaps the most rumored and biggest Bitcoin exchanging trades with double office exchanging straightforwardly and through the wallet. CoinBase was established in the year 2012 through the adventure finding of Y-Combinator and from that point forward it has quickly developed. It has numerous worthwhile services like various choices to store and pulls out currency, currency moves between two CoinBase are immediate, Wallet offices with different mark alternatives for safer exchanges, Bitcoin stores are safeguarded for any misfortune, and so on CoinBase has a wide assortment of installment accomplices in Europe and the US, who flawlessly permit the exchanges to be carried on through them. It has moderately low exchange charges and offers Bitcoin exchange alongside an enormous number of Altcoin exchanging also.

Bitfinex:

It is quite possibly the most exceptional exchanging trades and it especially fits the accomplished cryptographic money dealers. With high liquidity for Ethereum just as Bitcoin, this trade has better choices like utilizing, edge subsidizing, and numerous request exchanges. Aside from this Bitfinex offers the highlights of adaptable GUI, many request types, similar to restrict, quit, following stop, market, and so on.

Perhaps the biggest trade as far as volume exchanged Bitfinex offers pseudonymity for exchanges and just for a portion of the services it requires recognizable pieces of proof. The solitary downside with this trade is that it doesn't uphold the purchasing of Bitcoin or some other altcoin through fiat exchanges.

Kraken:

It is one of the biggest Bitcoin exchanging trades in terms of liquidity, euro crypto exchanging volumes, and exchanging figures of Canadian Dollars, USD and Yen. Kraken is the most regarded trade controlled through the strife of digital money exchanges and has figured out how to guard the measures of clients independent of different trades being hacked simultaneously.

With 14+ digital money exchanging offices, the client can store the fiat just as digital currency alongside a comparative limit with regards to withdrawals. However, it isn't appropriate for fledglings yet it has better security highlights and low exchange expenses comparative with CoinBase. A most significant factor for Kraken is that it is confided locally and has been quick to show the volumes and costs on Bloomberg Terminal.

Is Bitcoin Gathering Over?

The inflow of institutional money is deferred, and Bitcoin buying is as of now just an inflow of USDT tokens. The days when vivacious buyers augmented their charge cards to buy Bitcoin may be done. Undoubtedly, even the Korean business sectors have chilled off.

In any case, trading continues - this time, saved by the Tether (USDT) asset. From the outset sight, Bitcoin's worth levels are good, at $6,743.53. though altcoins slide, Bitcoin keeps up its position, and its worth strength stretched out again to 43.2% of the total market capitalization for all coins and tokens.

Printing USDT fit with the quick move-in Bitcoin starting in the mid-year of 2017. Nevertheless, as of now, every implantation of USDT also caused energized buying through any remaining possible methods. By and by, novices are either paying special mind to the sidelines, or most have lost the assumption that there are altogether the speedier increments to be made in crypto. In any case, for submitted merchants, using USDT is another wellspring of pay.

Regardless of the way that in the abundance of 2.7 billion USDT were made, few out of every odd one of them found their way into BTC trading. Starting in the no so distant past, the proposal of USDT in BTC trades was close and underneath 20%, with strong levels in Japanese Yen, US Dollar, Korean Won, and a couple of various financial guidelines. In any case, presently, the photograph changed immediately, completed the course a few days.

As demonstrated by data from CryptoCompare, more than 54% of all BTC trades are Tether exchanges, due to the immense proposal of Bitfinex trading. It has all the earmarks of being as of now the crypto markets have moved to a phase where all exchanges are internal, and the two or three years may see costs move simply considering the exercises of crypto insiders and not institutional specialists from the universe of the standard asset.

A large portion of a month earlier, Tether went into a lot of altcoins - and now, it seems gets are redirected into Bitcoin. While this may make certain at costs regardless of what you look like at it, it also infers that for new Bitcoin buyers, an offering by and by into the prosperity of fiat is, really, irksome, and they may end up with USDT tokens.

Advanced Currency

Cryptographic money is a digital currency. It is additionally called virtual currency. It is an advanced resource that handles its exchanges utilizing cryptography, cryptography is utilized imperviously and affirms the exchanges. Bitcoin was included in 2009 as the principal decentralized cryptographic money.

From that point onward, a wide range of cryptographic forms of the money went onto the market. These are normally known as Altcoins. These monetary forms utilize decentralized service as a stabilizer to concentrated advanced currency and focal financial systems.

Dispersed service utilizes Bitcoin's blockchain exchange data set like a paid record. An encryption gadget produces decentralized digital money at a predefined value, which is imparted to people in general. In unified banking and the Federal Reserve System, sheets of chiefs or governments deal with the allowing of money through printing units of money, and the trade is done with digital bankbooks.

Nonetheless, in decentralized cryptographic money, organizations or governments can't deliver new substances or offer help to different organizations, banks, or organizations that hold a resource.

Satoshi Nakamoto Group made the hidden specialized contraption for decentralized cryptographic forms of money. Just about 1,000 cryptographic forms of money were made by September 2017, the vast majority of them tantamount to Bitcoin.

In cryptographic money systems, security, respectability, and general records are kept up with the assistance of a group of commonly dubious gatherings known as excavators, whereby the overall population is approved by the utilization of their PC systems, and timestamp exchanges are kept up by a particular timestamp plot. Excavators, to protect the security of a digital currency record for financial reasons.

Most digital forms of money are continually limiting the creation of currency, covering the whole measure of money available for use and impersonating significant metals. In contrast to conventional monetary forms, which are held using money organizations, like holding currency in stock, digital currencies are hard to seize by law authorization.

This issue is because of the utilization of cryptographic technologies. Cryptographic forms of money like Bitcoin are aliases, additional items, for example, Zerocoinhave been recommended to give true secrecy.

Some obscure Persons or people utilized the title Satoshi Nakamoto and added Bitcoin in 2009, the primary advanced money. SHA-256, a cryptographic hash work, was utilized as a working plot in it. Namecoin used to be arranged in April 2011. Litecoin used to be delivered, in October 2011, Scrypt was the hash work in it. Cryptographic money, Peercoin utilized the crossover as work evidence. Particle didn't utilize blockchain, it utilizes the knot.

Based on an altered blockchain, The Divi Project grants easy purchasing and selling between monetary standards from the wallet and the capacity to utilize non-freely recognizable data for exchanges. Thereafter, numerous interesting cryptographic forms of money have been made, anyway, a couple has been fruitful, as they had been lack of specialized advancements.

This ATM was indistinguishable from bank ATMs anyway it examined the IDs, for example, identification or driver permit of the client with the assistance of scanners. Just about 1574 bitcoin ATMs had been mounted in unmistakable nations in 2017 with the normal of 3 ATMs had been snared each day in 2017.

The lawful height of digital forms of the money goes amiss vigorously from one country to another is as yet suffering in a considerable lot of them. Albeit a few nations have permitted their utilization and exchange, others have prohibited it. Also, different government establishments have limited bitcoins unexpectedly. In 2014 China Central Bank precluded the treatment of bitcoins by monetary foundations in China.

In Russia, nonetheless, cryptographic forms of money are legitimate, even though it is criminal to utilize different monetary standards to purchase products except the Russian ruble. The United States Internal Revenue Service permitted bitcoin to be dependent upon capital additions charge, on March 25, 2014, this decision explained the legitimateness of bitcoin.

If Amazon.com were a country, its income would make it about the 80th greatest GDP on the planet, and now it has its currency. As of late, proprietors of a Kindle Fire got a free store of 500 Amazon Coins to get their double citizenship launched.

Are Amazon Coins a Virtual Currency Like Bitcoin?

Will people discard the US dollar for the legitimate delicate of the United States of Amazon? No; the rollout of Amazon Coins is so for "a great many Kindle Fire applications, games and in-application things at Amazon.com or on your Kindle Fire" - not books or motion pictures.

And keeping in mind that bought coins never terminate, special coins got for nothing or as a component of another offer just keep going for a year. Then, the normal life expectancy of an electronic gadget these days is more limited than Napoleon dodging under a dwarf goat. For the present, in any case, if you ditch the Fire for an iPad, Amazon will keep your coins in its container.

In contrast to Bitcoin, the favored strategy for unknown exchanges for drug bargains and uncommon earth magnets disapproved of by the Consumer Product Safety Commission, there's no open trade market for Amazon Coins. Truth be told, Amazon says, "Coins can't be exchanged, moved for esteem, recovered for money or applied to some other record, but the degree legally necessary". Indeed, even Second Life Linden Dollars can be traded for Bitcoins, and afterward exchanged once more into currency on one of a few Bitcoin trades.

Amazon is selling their coins at a rebate - 500 coins for $4.80 up to 10,000 coins for $90.00 - and that appears to be a decent arrangement. At up to a 10% markdown, it resembles keeping away from the Internet deals charge that might be carried out later on if Congress gets everything it might want.

Differentiation this with Microsoft who likewise utilizes a point system on the Xbox Marketplace yet gives just 80 focuses per dollar. In case you're Microsoft, you give or offer focuses to purchase applications and games, in addition, to expand purchaser wallet-portion of different items, for example, Skype approaching which the focuses can be spent.

Google and Apple and Microsoft all have their application dissemination systems, and Amazon has their equipment stage Kindle as of now so why not? Amazon needs to extend a lot of the tablet market while pushing digital books, games stock, however, needs more applications grew, so actually like Microsoft's Xbox Marketplace point system, Amazon Coins serve to incent engineers to offer Fire forms and offer the income, relax the sticker stun of buys, in addition, to get shoppers guided into different contributions, for example, the reputed Amazon set-top box.

The main has a place with Bitcoin (BTC), which stays the market chief in all classes. Bitcoin has the greatest cost, the largest suspicion, the vast majority of the security (due to the amazing energy utilization of Bitcoin mining), the most celebrated brand character (the forks have attempted to be fitting), and the greater part of the improvement Active and normal. It is additionally the solitary piece to date that is addressed in the customary business sectors as Bitcoin fates exchanging on the American CME and CBOE.

Bitcoin stays the principle motor; The exhibition of any remaining parts exceptionally corresponds with the Bitcoin execution. I assume that the hole among Bitcoin and most-if, not any remaining parts will extend. Bitcoin has a few promising advancements in the pipeline that will before long be introduced as extra layers or delicate forks. Models are the

Flash system (LN), the tree, Schnorr marks Mimblewimbleund substantially more.

Specifically, we intend to open another scope of uses for Bitcoin, as it considers huge scope, microtransactions, and moment and secure payouts. LN is progressively steady as clients test their various conceivable outcomes with genuine Bitcoin. As it gets simpler to utilize, it very well may be dared to profit enormously from the selection of Bitcoin.

Exchange Bitcoins and Get the Most Out of It

This digital surge of currency that is clearing the worldwide financial backers isn't just getting simpler yet in addition more dangerous consistently. While it was at first a straightforward shared system for little exchanges, it is currently utilized for significant speculations and unfamiliar extravagance buys, which has presented more up-to-date techniques and employments. How can it truly function?

Bitcoin is currently very much like some other. It cannot exclusively be utilized to purchase and sell, however can be utilized for contributing and sharing, and can even be taken. While the underlying presentation of the technology accompanied a work area program, it would now be able to be straightforwardly worked through a cell phone application, which permits you to quickly purchase, sell, exchange, or even money your bitcoins for dollars.

Speculation with bitcoins has gotten exceptionally mainstream, with significant amounts of currency being placed inconsistently. For each exchange, remember certain achievements. The 'purchase low and sell high methodology isn't pretty much as effectively executed as said.

An extraordinary method to succeed quicker when you choose to exchange bitcoins, however, is to gain proficiency with the details. Like money ventures, there are currently a few bitcoin diagramming devices to record the advertising patterns and make forecasts to help you settle on speculation choices. Indeed, even as a fledgling, figuring out how to utilize diagramming instruments and how to peruse outlines can go far.

An ordinary graph will generally incorporate the initial value, the end value, the most exorbitant cost, the least cost, and the exchanging range, which are the fundamentals you need before making any deal or buy. Additionally, new financial backers will regularly immediately open unbeneficial positions. With this, nonetheless, recall that you need to pay a loan fee for like clockwork that the position is kept open, except for the initial 24 hours that are free. In this way, except if you have adequate equilibrium to cover the high-loan fee, don't keep any unfruitful position open for over 24 hours.

Bitcoin Brokers and the Growing Popularity of Bitcoins

Bitcoin dealers are progressively turning into a significant viewpoint with regards to exchanging bitcoin. When you get the correct merchant you will be a way to getting an incentive for your currency as they are regularly made at an anticipated and diminishing rate. Over the long run, the quantities of bitcoins made each year are regularly split consequently until their issuance ends totally to 21 million of those in presence. When it gets to this point, diggers are upheld solely by little exchange expenses.

Guideline

It is workable for the utilization of bitcoins to be directed similar way different instruments are managed. Actually like currency, they can be used for an assortment of purposes including both real and ill-conceived dependent on the laws inside a specific locale. Consequently, they are not quite the same as different devices or assets. Regardless, they can be exposed to assorted guidelines in each country viable.

In case of misfortune

If a client loses his/her wallet, the currency is frequently taken out from dissemination. By and by, bitcoins stay in the chain actually like others. Yet, lost bitcoins frequently stay lethargic uncertainly because no one can track down the private key(s) that would empower them to be utilized once more. In light of the guideline of interest and supply, when the market has less, the interest for those which are accessible will be high, which means expanded worth or costs of the ones which are accessible on the lookout.

Turning into a significant installment system

The system can deal with a few exchanges each second. In any case, the system isn't prepared to increase to the degree of Mastercard organizations. Work is in progress to raise the current constraints, other than the future prerequisites being notable. Since its initiation, each part of the system has been on a persistent pattern of development, specialization, and advancement. Furthermore, this interaction is required to remain similar route for various years to come. Besides, as the traffic develops, more clients of the system are required to utilize lightweight customers.

Bitcoins and criminal operations

Concerns are regularly raised that the system can be utilized to work with criminal operations. In any case, these highlights exist with wire and money moves which are grounded and generally utilized. Utilization will be exposed to the very guidelines that have been set up inside existing monetary systems. The system is probably not going to keep criminal examinations from being led. For the most part, it isn't unprecedented for significant forward leaps to be viewed as being dubious sometime before their benefits are surely known.

The blockchain is an online decentralized public record of all digital exchanges that have occurred. It is advanced currency's likeness to a high road bank's record that records exchanges between two gatherings. Similarly, as our cutting-edge banking system couldn't work without the way to record the trades of fiat currency between people, so too could a digital network not capacity without the trust that comes from the capacity to precisely record the trading of advanced money between parties.

It is decentralized as in, dissimilar to a conventional bank which is the sole holder of an electronic expert record of its record holder's reserve funds the blockchain record is divided between all people from the organization and isn't dependent upon the terms and states of a specific monetary establishment or country. What of it? For what reason is this desirable over our present financial system?

A decentralized financial organization guarantees that by sitting outside of the evermore associated current monetary system one can moderate the dangers of being important for it when things turn out badly. The 3 principal dangers of an incorporated financial system that were featured because of the 2008 monetary emergency are credit, liquidity, and operational disappointment. In the US alone since 2008 there have been 504 bank disappointments because of indebtedness, there being 157 out of 2010 alone.

Ordinarily, such a breakdown doesn't imperil the record holder's reserve funds because of government/public support and protection for the initial not many hundred thousand dollars/pounds, the bank's resources generally being consumed

24

by another monetary foundation yet the effect of the breakdown can cause vulnerability and momentary issues with getting to reserves.

Since a decentralized system like the Bitcoin network isn't subject to a bank to work with the exchange of assets between 2 gatherings but instead depends on its huge number of clients to approve exchanges it is stronger to such disappointments, it has however many reinforcements as there are people from the organization to guarantee exchanges keep on being approved in case of one person from the organization 'falling'.

A decentralized system isn't dependent on this sort of foundation, it as opposed to being founded on the joined handling force of its huge number of clients which guarantees the capacity to increase as essential, an issue in any piece of the system not making the organization come to a standstill.

How Bitcoin Will Promote Latin American Growth?
Latin America has gotten a mainland spotlight on a worldwide scale with smothered European development and an Asia-Pacific locale that has effectively been invited into the worldwide monetary discussion. Elective monetary forms will transform Latin America and it will influence the two sides in an alternate style.

Bitcoin's Impact on state-arranged Economies
In these state-arranged economies, there are currency controls. Venezuela and Argentina are notorious for their cost controls. Brazil's service's impact on the economy comes from its exorbitant impact, conceivable defilement issues, and inflationary concerns. Business people, financial backers, and customary people will be looking to the commercial center to address their issues. Apportioning, formality, significant expenses, and conceivable reconnaissance are related to these

state-arranged economies. Bitcoin and digital forms of money will address the issues of numerous that approach the internet.

Contending universally in nations that wish to be more isolated accompanies negative implications, yet the utilization of the internet and the capacity to execute in a conceivably untraced style in a worldwide commercial center will empower cutthroat evaluating for residents to get the labor and products required. Venezuelans will want to purchase bathroom tissue from unfamiliar sources without utilizing currency that is as a rule degraded.

Venezuelans will likewise have the chance to take part in the business ventures while still in Venezuela to subsidize their undertakings and conceivable absconding to different nations like Colombia. More than 26% of Venezuelans utilize the internet consistently. Venezuela has not sifted the internet right now and buying Bitcoin is undeniably safer than clutching Bolivar.

Bitcoin use could take the public authority's solid handle on the economy away by delivering its quality pointless by receiving the private money. Fewer assessment incomes can be gathered, a general population that is outfitted monetarily and conceivably in a real sense (you might have purchased anything on Silk Road), and diminished impact from political pioneers and authorities as digital money utilization gets viral. This perspective can be applied to Venezuela-light in Argentina, which is an economy with a ton of possibilities.

Bitcoin's Specific Role in the Economic Growth of the Pacific Countries

Business venture as portrayed in the past area is on a more modest level than what might be in Mexico, Chile, Colombia, and Peru. Colombia and Mexico have urban areas that have desires to worldwide parts in the digital space. Drawing in business from Europe, Canada, and the United States would be simpler with lower trade and exchange expenses.

Charge cards and PayPal place exchange expenses on clients wishing to make worldwide exchanges and this charge would be decreased. Latin American reevaluating can encounter development as call focuses, improvement, and configuration firms, and self-employed entities can seriously offer as they do now, however they would have the option to acknowledge Bitcoin and other digital currencies and this will drive in more business.

It's anything but a trend, it involves making a simpler and less expensive exchange. Fewer obstructions to making the buy will make the deal and it can help Latin American organizations be worldwide, which can prompt Venture Capital development.

Bitcoin will prompt more prominent worldwide deals for Latin America and empower financial development. The advantages are diverse for these nations as the requirement for steadiness isn't squeezing, yet rather these nations have a voracious craving for development. Business ventures, contending worldwide, lower exchange charges, value-based security, cutthroat offering, improved financial turn of events, and changing discernments are on the whole advantages of receiving digital forms of money in these nations.

A startup in Medellin or Cartagena can contend with a firm in Toronto and another firm in Indianapolis for a service contract. Eliminating the obstructions of ethnicity from the exchange to focus exclusively on the services gave and costs included are a significant advantage.

Shoppers win too in these nations as they would acquire buying power since certain things are costlier in their homegrown business sectors than unfamiliar business sectors. Ex-taps and foreigners can send currency to relatives in their local country in a straightforward, reasonable, fast, and secure style. This can help support nearby economies.

Bitcoin and other digital currencies help make the world a more modest spot very much like how air travel, the internet, broadcast communications, and web-based media have done.

Bitcoin Chapter 2 – Bitcoin Marketplace

About Bitcoin

In case you're here, you've known about Bitcoin. It has been one of the greatest successive news features in the course of the most recent year or something like that - like a pyramid scheme, the finish of account, the introduction of really worldwide money, as the apocalypse, or as a technology that has improved the world. Yet, what is Bitcoin? To put it plainly, you could say Bitcoin is the principal decentralized arrangement of currency utilized for online exchanges, yet it will most likely be helpful to burrow somewhat more profound.

We as a whole know, all in all, what 'currency is and what it is utilized for. The main issue that saw in currency use before Bitcoin identifies with it being brought together and constrained by a solitary element - the unified financial framework. Bitcoin was imagined in 2008/2009 by an obscure maker who passes by the nom de plume 'Nakamoto' to welcome decentralization to currency on a worldwide scale.

The thought is that the currency can be exchanged across worldwide lines with no trouble or charges, the governing rules would be conveyed across the whole globe (instead of simply on the records of private companies or governments), and currency would turn out to be more equitable and similarly available to all.

Bitcoin is a digital currency that has drawn in a ton of media consideration throughout the most recent few years and keeps on doing as such. Bitcoin was set up by an unknown gathering or person in 2009, who utilized the nom de plume Nakamoto, after whom the littlest unit of Bitcoin currency is named. It is the first and ostensibly the most broadly known cryptographic money. Initially just important to the web tip-top, Bitcoin has acquired more extensive allure as of late and deserves admiration by its own doing on the unfamiliar trade.

How does Bitcoin work?

The better subtleties of how Bitcoin functions can be precarious to get a handle on, because it isn't under focal control as a traditional currency, yet rather every exchange is however endorsed by an organization of clients. There are no coins and no notes, no bullion held in a vault, however, the Bitcoin supply is limited, it will stop at 21 million. At regular intervals, 25 Bitcoins are found by Bitcoin "diggers", and like clockwork, the number of Bitcoins delivered will split until the cutoff is reached. This means that there will be no further arrival of Bitcoins after 2140.

How did Bitcoin start?

The idea of Bitcoin, and digital currency, by and large, was begun in 2009 by Satoshi, an obscure scientist. The justification for its creation was to settle the issue of centralization in the utilization of currency which depended on banks and PCs, an issue that numerous PC researchers weren't content with. Accomplishing decentralization has endeavored since the last part of the 90s without progress, so when Satoshi distributed a paper in 2008 answering, it was overwhelmingly invited. Today, Bitcoin has become a recognizable currency for web clients and has led to a huge number of 'altcoins' (non-Bitcoin digital currencies).

How would I contribute?

In the first place, you need to open a record with an exchanging stage and make a wallet; you can discover a few models via scanning Google for 'Bitcoin exchanging stage' - they for the most part have names including 'coin', or 'market'. After going along with one of these stages, you click on the resources and afterward click on crypto to pick your ideal monetary standards. There are a ton of pointers on each stage that is very significant, and you ought to make certain to notice them before contributing.

How is Bitcoin made?

Bitcoin is made through a cycle called mining. Very much like paper currency is made through printing, and gold is mined from the beginning, is made by 'mining'. Mining includes tackling complex numerical issues in regards to blocks utilizing PCs and adding them to a public record. At the point when it started, a straightforward CPU (like that in your home PC) was every one of the one expected to mine, nonetheless, the degree of trouble has expanded altogether, and now you will require specific equipment, including very good quality Graphics Processing Unit (GPUs), to remove Bitcoin.

Purchase and hold

While mining is the surest and, as it were, the easiest approach to procure Bitcoin, there is an excessive amount of hustle included, and the expense of power and concentrated PC equipment makes it unavailable to the greater part of us. To stay away from this, make it simple for yourself, simply input the sum you need from your bank and snap "purchase', at that point pause for a minute and watch as your speculation expands as indicated by the value change. This is called trading and happens on many trade stages accessible today, with the capacity to exchange between a wide range of fiat monetary standards (USD, AUD, GBP, and so forth) and distinctive crypto coins (Ethereum, Bitcoin, Litecoin, and so on)

Bitcoin as Shares

There are additional associations set up to permit you to purchase partakes in organizations that put resources into Bitcoin - these organizations do the to and fro exchanging, and you simply put resources into them and sit tight for your monthly benefits. These organizations just pool advanced currency from various financial backers and contribute for their benefit.

Exchanging Bitcoin

If you know about stocks, bonds, or Forex trades, you will comprehend crypto-exchanging without any problem. There are Bitcoin intermediaries like e-social exchanging, FXTM markets.com, and numerous others that you can browse. The stages give you Bitcoin-fiat or Fiat-Bitcoin currency sets, model BTC-USD means exchanging Bitcoins for U.S. Dollars. Keep your eyes on the value changes to track down the ideal pair as per value changes; the stages give cost among different markers to give you appropriate exchanging tips.

A part of the principal features of Bitcoins are:

It is exclusively an advanced type of money, and you can't supplant them with its actual structure. It utilizes shared technology and isn't constrained by any focal specialists. The exchanges are done however among the elaborate gatherings and the organization, with no mediation from the national banks. It is liberated from any kind of impedances or controls by the administrations since it is completely decentralized.

The top cap of giving Bitcoins is restricted to 21 million, which is normal of only 25 coins being dug for like clockwork. The speed of mining has eased back down significantly more over the most recent 2 years.

Bitcoins are somewhat more unpredictable to comprehend when contrasted with customary monetary standards like dollars. In this manner, you should acquire some specialized information about them, particularly before utilizing them for internet exchanging.

Bitcoins have constraints in acknowledgment since they are not generally acknowledged at all stores. However, the possibility of acknowledgment improves its developing prevalence. This cryptographic money has made considerable progress since its presentation in 2009.

One of the disadvantages of Bitcoins is that the exchanges will for the most part take around 10 minutes to finish, which is not normal for the customary monetary forms where the exchanges can be finished right away. Also, the exchanges are irreversible, and the discounting should be possible just if the beneficiary consents to do as such.

Bitcoin permits you to make exchanges mysteriously since you won't need to give your name or address. As referenced above, it works with the shared framework.

Why to put resources into Bitcoin?

As should be obvious, putting resources into Bitcoin requests that you have some essential information on the money, as clarified previously. Similarly, as with all speculations, it means hazard! Whether to contribute relies completely upon the person.

In any case, if I somehow managed to offer guidance, I would instruct in the favor regarding putting resources into Bitcoin with an explanation that, Bitcoin continues to develop - although there has been one huge win and fail period, almost certainly, Cryptocurrencies will keep on expanding in esteem throughout the following 10 years.

The cost has verifiably been exceptionally unpredictable, with critical pinnacles and droops at spans. As of late, the cost of a Bitcoin jumped up more than 10-crease in only two months. In 2013 a few Bitcoin Millionaires were made for the time being the point at which the worth of their Bitcoin wallets expanded drastically.

If you as of now hold some bitcoins in your advanced wallet or are considering trying things out, at that point you truly should keep up to speed with the Bitcoin News. Exchanging Bitcoin is an undeniably popular option or extra to traditional unfamiliar trade exchanging and is filling in help as more specialists dive in.

Notwithstanding the steadily falling pace of Bitcoin revelation, the interest in Bitcoin news proceeds. There is a genuine and steady interest for up to the moment, dependable data about its worth. Bitcoin got a solid underwriting from PayPal as of late which will positively reinforce trust in its believability as a dependable option in contrast to a traditional bank card or money exchanges online and on the high road.

This may go some approach to assuage the pundits of Bitcoin, who guarantee that the framework used to support or approve exchanges, called Blockchain, and is uncertain and defenseless against assault by programmers.

Advantage and Disadvantages of Bitcoin

It is a type of digital currency. Nobody has any command over it. Being digital money, it isn't printed like rupees, euros, or dollars. However, they are delivered and made by people for different exchanges. Progressively, an ever-increasing number of organizations are starting to utilize it for different kinds of exercises.

This type of money is for the most part made by programming that can take care of complex numerical issues. After having said something regarding this digital money, the time has come to discuss its advantages and disadvantages so that people can choose whether they ought to let it all out.

Pros

1: He will be in charge of the currency while utilizing this money. He isn't hampered by the special times of the year and different snags while doing exchanges with it.

2: It is feasible to send and get currency at some random time. The time and distance elements won't limit the client when he utilizes this money.

3: Merchants become unequipped for charging additional expenses on anything covertly. Subsequently, they are compelled to converse with the clients before imposing any charges on the exchanges.

4: The clients can finish the exchanges without uncovering any close-to-home data.

5: All the exchanges utilizing this advanced would be protected in the Internet network as the clients can scramble it.

6: Since the exchanges utilizing Bitcoin happen online, every one of them is all around recorded. Thus, anyone can see the square of exchanges. Nonetheless, the personal data would in any case be inaccessible to other people. Consequently, it would be a straightforward exchange

7: Since there is no restricting of person data with exchanges, dealers get insurance from potential misfortunes regardless of whether extortion happens.

8: The Bitcoin-based exchanges are either not chargeable or draw in extremely low expenses. Regardless of whether charged, that exchange gets need in the organization and gets executed quickly.

Cons

1: To get the message out about Bitcoin, organizing is essential. As of now, a couple of organizations can utilize this digital currency.

2: This currency network isn't known to people. Consequently, they need to think about this advanced money.

3: Due to the tremendous interest in this digital money, it's worth continues evolving day by day. It would settle just when the interest balances out on the lookout.

4: Currently, the exchanges dependent on this currency are profoundly unstable as just a predetermined number of coins are accessible.

6: Since this digital currency framework is in its earliest stages state, very little programming is accessible in the market to make it a protected exchange.

No focal organization can handle the inventory of Bitcoin, in contrast to fiat monetary standards or even materials like gold. The world can just at any point see a sum of 21 million Bitcoins in presence. Like any new problematic development, Bitcoin has a wildly steadfast center gathering of allies and devotees who are enthusiastic about the thought.

They are the ones who take it forward and spread the thought and take it to a higher level. Bitcoin has a lot of lovers who are amped up for the thought and how it can shape the fate of account, giving the influence of currency back to the majority rather than under focal control. It isn't only a passing prevailing fashion. Bitcoin is staying put.

Business people are taking their risks and building extraordinary organizations around this thought. Investment reserves are starting to help projects that rotate around Bitcoin (Coinbase just raised a $5 million endeavor store from the absolute best VCs, including the group that sponsored Tumblr). There are a lot of situations, dark swan, and in any case where Bitcoins can turn into a prevailing power in the monetary business.

There are a lot of pessimistic situations you can consider where Bitcoin will hold its value and worth as excessive inflation burns through the fiat currency of a feeble focal government (there has been at any rate one recorded case in Argentina where a person sold his home for Bitcoin). Nonetheless, that is in effect excessively negative. Indeed, even without anything awful occurring, Bitcoin can joyfully live close by the conventional monetary forms of the world.

Probably the best benefits of Bitcoin are acknowledged wasteful business sectors. It very well may be separated into a hundred million sections, each called a satoshi, instead of fiat which normally can be separated distinctly into 100 sections. Likewise, exchanges over this organization are free or now and again need a little exchange expense to instigate the excavators. By little, we are discussing not exactly a 10th of a percent. Contrast this with the 2-4% expense charged regularly by the Visa organizations and you being to perceive any reason why this idea is so alluring.

So since you're persuaded that Bitcoin is staying put since a long time ago arrived behind schedule, to utilize this? It is as yet in the beginning phases of advancement and there is a lot of where you can make some Bitcoin. Spigots, for example, are upheld exclusively by promoting and manual human tests and don't have any catch - you enter your wallet id and you get free Bitcoins.

There are a few different ideas from the Get-Paid-To world deciphered and made particularly for the Bitcoin economy. For example, there are a few manners by which you can take reviews, watch videos, and visit sponsor sites, all in return for some Bitcoins.

There doesn't need to be a genuine least payout and in any event, when there is, it is normally exceptionally insignificant. To take an interest in the Bitcoin economy, you shouldn't be a specialized master or even dig profound into the activities of the currency. There are a few administrations you can use to make the cycle as straightforward as could be expected. It is all dependent upon you to go out on a limb and stay in the game for the since quite a while ago run.

The True Story of the Bitcoin Market and Its Phenomenal Course

Bitcoin is currently considered to be the preeminent installment technique for online trade, enthusiastic observers of cryptographic forms of money believe this reality to be an intense walk on the path of account saw on an all-inclusive scale. Specialists, nonetheless, flash a new discussion around and on the issue of Bitcoin, basically the way that most purchasers in the Bitcoin market are a lot of examiners.

Bitcoin is an ideal impression of how digital forms of money can accept a shape in the approaching time, and business people should consider a bigger viewpoint. The monstrous prevalence and the steadily mounting cost are transitory, yet managing the fundamentals concerning Bitcoin and its minor rivals will prompt an ideal pondering and that will decide its approaching future.

Cryptographic money requires a competitor to the crown. The technology of Bitcoin is dreary, this is both unsafe and captivating simultaneously, and Bitcoin is a pioneer. Just 21 million Bitcoins can at any point be mined, expansion is anything but a potential choice, and cryptographic money can expect innumerable headings. Digital currencies like Litecoin are making strides. These digital monetary forms furnish buyers with examples of financial development and reflect swelling too.

Ongoing Bitcoin news demonstrates that organizations are attempting to foster contenders, to develop an answer for worldwide money-related exchanges by advanced monetary standards. Unpredictable Bitcoin, which is to some degree satisfactory or questionable by huge and independent ventures the same, even fuel the requirement for a stable digital currency for smoother exchanges.

Bitcoin is a stand-out. Exposure is the sole justification for its doubtful achievement. Customers can want to get it when they see the Bitcoin Charts, requests take off however aims are as yet unidentified. They are yet to get a handle on its importance and discover great utilization of it after they've effectively made a stride of feeling free to gain it. Albeit a currency, Bitcoin, with its sheer unpredictability is to some degree considered as gold by this world. Crashes and discussions might involve the past, however surely not for its natural worth.

There isn't anything amiss with advancing with digital forms of money, however, an over-the-top promotion around one isn't sound. Information can even affirm that a major level of spent Bitcoins is exchanged through betting elements. Interest triggers the inclination to purchase this unpredictable advanced currency; customers are tempted by the rising course of Bitcoin esteem and are consumed by it.

Misunderstandings do occur with digital money. A decentralized, open-source element, for example, Bitcoin is, set off a rage among its makers to assemble something extraordinary. Currency and assets weren't a thing of worry with them. The Bitcoin cost has, strangely, expanded as it got rumored step by step.

As the unpredictability of the currency is affirmed by its fast ascents and plunges, and the component of illiquidity for purchasers is an irrefutable issue. A progressive joy pulled in the absolute first Bitcoin takers. However, someplace simultaneously, something critical is getting lost, something that could follow or go with a digital currency like a shadow, the broad use for working with any kind of exchanges.

Correlation Between Gold and Bitcoin

In certain spots, gold appears to have a more significant spot in the monetary world. Then again, a few groups start to consider Bitcoin to be a legitimate technique to hold our investment funds. This permits us to shop and perform other everyday exchanges. For normal purchasers, Bitcoin and other cryptographic money appear to give an applicable other option. It is most likely a happy opportunity to make a correlation between gold and Bitcoin and Ethereum (other digital money).

People have been utilizing gold as a kind of currency since centuries prior; while Bitcoin has been around just barely longer than 10 years. Albeit the idea has gone through some developing interaction, gold has an unavoidable impact on the lookout. Bitcoin guarantees constant upgrades in accommodation, security, and usefulness. Specialists have contrasted the present status of Bitcoin and the Internet in the early and mid-1990s.

Advocates of Bitcoin contend that virtually all headways identified with gold have effectively occurred as seen by the mass acknowledgment of any actual gold bullion items since centuries prior. Truth be told, some organization acquisitions have been performing utilizing gold as money. They simply don't believe that the public authority will not go into out-of-control inflation.

The possibility of gold versus Bitcoin is a significant contention worth racking. Maybe than picking one of them; a considerable lot of us would like to utilize a mix of them to exploit the more desirable characteristics of each. Truth be told, we have seen a concurrence among Bitcoin and gold, as "Casascius coins. This the main occurrence of Bitcoin and gold meeting up and it will not be the last. Ethereum another digital money is at $1,549.00. It's typically best mined with Radeon designs cards x 5 or 6 set up on racks for the ideal association. Lan links permit it to dig at high rates for a benefit overpower utilization.

Paper currency is our answer for improving dissemination and gold is our predecessor's answer for protecting the worth of the money. The metal is less influenced by expansion since it is significantly costlier than paper or other modest metals. Furthermore, cryptographic money is the new innovative stuff to give dependability during exchanges, with the agelessness and exactness of a Swiss watch. Despite the analysis, Bitcoin and other digital currencies will keep on speaking to numerous people because of their unmistakable benefits, particularly when contrasted with traditional monetary standards, for example, paper currency which gets expanded and is frequently lost, spent, or taken.

It depends on prompt, direct P2P (distributed) exchanges to keep away from lumbering and costly electronic installment frameworks. Over the long run, financial backers would find that Bitcoin conveys an improved store of significant worth than any sequentially printed level monetary forms. The Bitcoin convention sets a boundary for the number of bitcoins accessible at one time.

There will consistently be 21 million bitcoins and the framework appears to be more genuine than even the US dollar now and again. With Bitcoin and other digital currencies, purchasers could get expanded monetary protection; although there are worries that the public authority will quietly take advantage of the framework with consistent monetary checking.

Bitcoins were at first considered as a promoting contrivance, yet now it is an undeniable currency, which is upheld by numerous organizations and numerous people also invest their energy exchanging bitcoins. Numerous people purchase and sell bitcoins to get benefits and numerous organizations use them as the installment choice to make installments more flexible and simpler for the clients. Watched by blockchain technology and the extent of being mysterious is one of the significant reasons why bitcoin exchanges have gotten so popular.

A portion of the significant advantages of utilizing bitcoins in the current market are examined underneath:

No swelling

One of the significant issues with typical monetary forms and protecting them is that the market is powerless against expansion now and then. However, bitcoins have no danger of expansion as there is no restriction of currency and however there is no danger of a decline in the buying force of the clients.

41

Hence, there is no danger of expansion even with a limitless money age and this is probably the best motivation behind why bitcoins can be protected.

Convenience

Probably the most concerning issue with worldwide exchanges with regards to typical money is the pace of trade and that each nation has its currency, however making the whole cycle troublesome and very bothering. However, with regards to bitcoins, people can undoubtedly do any kind of worldwide exchange without trading the monetary forms with the nearby bank and discovering the swapping scale. All that should be done is to utilize the memory card and the bitcoin record to execute a certain bitcoin sum to someone else's record absent a lot of exertion.

Diminished extortion

Dissimilar to credit and charge cards which reveal a client's monetary and personal subtleties to the traders, bitcoin can be executed without that danger. One doesn't need to give any kind of close-to-home subtleties while purchasing or selling bitcoins, hence being careful from monetary fakes and dangers. Likewise, there is zero chance of bitcoin hacking as it is advanced money without a hackable impression and forestalls any kind of focused information penetrate.

Fewer charges and fast exchanges

With regards to bitcoins, the exchanges are done within 24 to 48 hours as the whole cycle is done through digital interaction and absent a lot of deterrents. Also, the exchange expenses of the bitcoins are substantially less than the typical card or bank exchanges, in this manner making it an entirely suitable alternative for little or medium-sized organizations.

Being a famous type of currency, bitcoins are acquiring overall praise these days, thus, numerous people have shown their premium in getting them. Albeit numerous monetary heads are recommending people not to enjoy this type of digital money, because of its fluctuating worth, yet it is being acknowledged at a high speed. To buy bitcoins, one can join with the wallet framework for nothing by topping off every one of the online subtleties or download a portable application and begin putting resources into them.

When people have it straightforward financial installment techniques could be utilized to trade them. Notwithstanding, since security is the great factor these wallets must stay safe and it is because of this explanation one ought to have the option to pick a bitcoin administration, for example, the coin base wallets that are of exclusive requirements and simple to utilize.

Albeit an online wallet is an advantageous strategy for purchasing bitcoins there are a few different alternatives, for example, choosing a bitcoin broker. It is likewise imperative to pick the correct one as there are tricksters and one ought to be cautious about them. Though various setup trades offer wallet administrations to the clients while searching for a bitcoin wallet framework the person ought to settle on the one that has a multi-signature office. The clients can likewise utilize the bitcoin trade search in particular PCs or cell phones and by putting some broad data, for example, composing one's nation name the person can discover a wide scope of accessible trades across the world to look at its momentum status.

The clients can likewise utilize the fluid currency they have since there are different alternatives accessible in the commercial center, for example, neighborhood bitcoin administrations that assist the clients to trade them with currency. Such regions permit the clients to visit the closest bank office for keeping the money sum and get the bitcoins after some time.

Numerous people accept that bitcoins address another period of advanced money and frequently get mistaken for them. However, since the bitcoin chain framework is completely modernized it is very straightforward and simple to purchase and utilize them particularly they are damnation modest with regards to worldwide exchanges. Since trades request an assortment of installment cycles, for example, credit or check cards, the buyers can likewise purchase online by opening a record based on the separate geological area.

When the trades get the installments after check they would save the bitcoins in the interest of the people and submit them in the particular wallets. For this, they charge a few expenses. The whole cycle may be tedious. Numerous people who are figuring out how to purchase bitcoins can likewise utilize the PayPal strategy for monetary collaborations.

Steps to Get $10 of Free Bitcoin, Easy and Simple

At this point, you've likely found out about Bitcoin - there are accounts of people making a huge number of dollars short-term with this and other Crypto-monetary forms. The principal things to think about purchasing Bitcoin are that there are a few fundamental approaches to buy it, and it isn't so convoluted to do as such. The fundamental two different ways to buy Bitcoin are through a representative or a trade. Look at the Coinbase trade - they're perhaps the greatest trade, have a perfect and straightforward interface, are open by applications on different portable and PC stages, and offer you US$10 of free Bitcoin to begin.

There are different trades that I have attempted, and that function admirably - BTCMarkets, and Coinspot, to name a couple which is both acceptable - however just Coinbase has the $10 startup reward.

Bitcoin is the most well-known and greatest digital currency on the planet concerning showcasing capitalization and the portion of the overall industry where there are no go-betweens to deal with the exchanges. Microsoft Co-originator, Bill Gates has a great deal of confidence in Bitcoin to the purpose of saying, "Bitcoin is an innovative masterpiece."

As per Leon Louw, a Nobel Peace Prize candidate, each educated person has to know in any event about bitcoin since it can get one of the world's hugest turns of events. One can purchase bitcoins simply from other bitcoin clients using commercial centers or through trades, and one pays for them through hard money, credit or charge cards, electronic wire moves, other digital currencies, PayPal, et al.

How Then Can One Buy Bitcoins?
Get a Bitcoin Wallet

Diverse bitcoin wallets give differing levels of safety, and you can pick the security level that turns out best for your exchanges. The most popular wallet alternatives are

Where to Buy Bitcoins

• **Localbitcoins: -** This is the essential site for masterminding up close and personal exchanges and costs arranged. Its escrow administration has made the site famous since it adds a layer of assurance for the purchaser and the vendor with a trust score of A.

• **Bitquick: -** This site is also novice cordial permitting clients to purchase and acknowledge installments for bitcoins using hard currency just as the bank moves. It has a trust rating of B.

• **Wesellcrypto:** - This site positions high, and it is novice agreeable. It has a trust rating of B+, and you can purchase bitcoins using your PayPal account.

With bitcoins, you can secretly purchase stock; make less expensive worldwide installments since Bitcoins are not dependent upon guidelines from any country. The bitcoin market is unpredictable and more people are getting them wanting to make a benefit when the cost goes up

"Zero-affirmation" exchanges are quick, where the trader acknowledges the danger, which is as yet not supported by the Bitcoin blockchain. If the trader needs endorsement, the exchange requires 10 minutes.

In Bitcoin exchanges, the expenses are normally low, and at times, it is free. Bitcoin is decentralized, so no focal authority can remove a rate from your stores. When you exchange Bitcoins, they are no more. You can't recover them without the beneficiary's assent. In this way, it gets hard to submit chargeback misrepresentation, which is regularly capable by people with Visas.

If you don't have a clue what Bitcoin is, do a touch of exploration online, and you will get bounty. Moreover, Bitcoin exchanges should be private, which is mysterious. Most curiously, Bitcoins have no genuine presence; they exist just in PC programming, as a kind of computer-generated reality.

Bitcoin Chapter 3 All About Bitcoin Cryptocurrency

Bitcoin Cryptocurrency is humming everywhere in the world, regardless of whether you are online or in any media. It is quite possibly the most energizing and craziest thing that happened that appears over the most recent couple of years as it were. All the more critically, you can acquire an amazing return by bitcoins exchanging or you can save it as long as possible. You might be found out about Stocks, Commodities, Forex, and now new money called Bitcoin exchanging that impacts incredibly on our lives. In this current novice's manual for Bitcoin digital money, you will become acquainted with the A B C of Bitcoin.

About Bitcoin Cryptocurrency

The development of Bitcoin is as yet not known yet a paper was distributed in October 2008 under the pen name Nakamoto held from Japan. His character is at this point unclear and accepted to have around 1,000,000 bitcoins esteemed at more than USD 6 billion as of September 2017. Bitcoin is advanced money prevalently known as a digital currency and is liberated from any geological limit. It isn't managed by any administration and all you need is an internet connection. As a novice, Bitcoin technology may befuddle you and somewhat intense to think about it.

In any case, I will help you burrow it more profound and how you can likewise do your first Bitcoin exchanging quietly. Bitcoin Cryptocurrency deals with blockchain technology which is a digital public account and shared by anybody on the planet. You will discover your exchanges here at whatever point you do any Bitcoin exchanging and anybody can utilize the account to check it. The exchange done will be straightforward and is checked by blockchain. Bitcoin and other cryptographic forms of money are portions of a blockchain and are a great technology that sudden spikes in demand for the web as it were.

Key Terms Related to Bitcoin Cryptocurrency

Before you are prepared to possess your first Bitcoin, it is smarter to realize the key terms identified with bitcoins. It is also named BTC which is a piece of bitcoin and 1 bitcoin approaches 1 Million pieces. With the rise of bitcoins, some other elective digital forms of money also developed. They are prominently called Altcoins and incorporate Ethereum(ETH), Litecoin(LTC), Ripple(XRP), Monero(MXR), and numerous others. XBT and BTC are the same things and are generally contracted for bitcoin. Mining is a new term utilized a great deal and it is a cycle done by PC equipment for the Bitcoin organizations.

Things You Can Do with Bitcoin

You will want to exchange, execute, acknowledge and store bitcoin. It also ensures your security that may get spilled online while utilizing Visas. It is amazingly secure and no one can seize or take coins. Because of its straightforwardness in the framework, it is likewise impractical to control given the common public account.

You can check exchanges from any place and whenever. The request is probably going to ascend as the complete creation of bitcoins is to be restricted to 21 million in particular. Japan has effectively sanctioned it and different nations may follow it soon and the cost may climb further. I will cover more on Bitcoins exhaustively in the impending days where you will learn extraordinary stuff about bitcoin exchanging. You can remark on your perspectives and ask anything pertinent to bitcoins.

What Is a Cryptocurrency?

Digital money or cryptographic money is a virtual currency that serves to trade labor and products through an arrangement of electronic exchanges without going through any go-between. The principal digital money that began exchanging was Bitcoin in 2009, and from that point forward numerous others have arisen, with different highlights like Litecoin, Ripple, Dogecoin, and others.

When contrasting a digital currency and the currency in the ticket, the thing that matters is that:

They are decentralized: they are not constrained by the bank, the public authority, and any monetary establishment

They're International: everybody's show with them

They are protected: your coins are yours and from no one else, it is kept in a person wallet with non-adaptable codes that lone you know

It has no go-betweens: exchanges are completed from one person to another

Fast exchanges: to send currency to another country they charge revenue and frequently it requires days to affirm; with digital forms of money a couple of moments.

Irreversible exchanges.

Bitcoins and some other virtual money can be traded for any world currency

It can't be faked because they are scrambled with a modern cryptographic framework

In contrast to monetary standards, the worth of electronic monetary standards is dependent upon the most established guideline of the market: market interest. "Presently it has a worth of more than 1000 dollars and like stocks, this worth can go up or down the organic market.

Bitcoin is the principal digital money made by Satoshi Nakamoto in 2009. He chose to dispatch another money. Its quirk is that you can just perform tasks inside the organization of organizations. Bitcoin alludes to both the currency and the convention and the red P2P on which it depends.

Bitcoin is a virtual and elusive currency. That is, you can't contact any of its structures similarly as with coins or bills, however, you can utilize it as a method for installment similarly to these. In certain nations, you can adapt with an electronic check card page that brings in currency trades with digital forms of money like XAPO.

Without a doubt, what makes Bitcoin unique about conventional monetary standards and other virtual methods for installment like Amazon Coins, Action Coins, is decentralization. Bitcoin isn't constrained by any administration, organization, or monetary element, either state or private, like the euro, constrained by the Central Bank or the Dollar by the Federal Reserve of the United States.

In Bitcoin control the genuine, by implication by their exchanges, clients through trades P2 P (Point to Point or Point to Point). This design and the absence of control make it inconceivable for any position to control its worth or cause swelling by delivering a greater amount. Its creation and worth depend on the law of the organic market. Another fascinating subtlety with regards to Bitcoin has a constraint of 21 million coins, which will be reached in 2030.

Bitcoin is a shiny new sort of capital or money. It looks like the US Dollar, the Euro, or the Peso, then again, actually it isn't constrained by any single organization or government. Maybe then being controlled by a solitary body, bitcoin is a decentralized shared currency, implying that it lives on the PC of everybody that works with it. (Equivalent to the actual web.) Given that it's decentralized, nobody can ruin the commercial center by delivering more bitcoins into the course and no divider road investor is filling one's pockets by remaining in the focal point of each request.

The advantages of bitcoin are that exchanges happen in a flash and don't need an exchange expense - except if the person beginning the exchange chooses to pay one. Since no one controls the bitcoin network, there are PCs throughout the world who help affirm every exchange that occurs - this cycle is designated "mining."To boost these "excavators" to help confirm every one of the exchanges, the bitcoin network awards bitcoins to diggers incidentally. By and by, 25 bitcoins are remunerated in a type of lottery framework at regular intervals. The program behind bitcoin manages this lottery and it's open-source so everybody can see it.

The rate that bitcoins are granted will divide to 12.5 in 2017 and afterward cut down the middle again at regular intervals until the last bitcoins are remunerated in 2140. Then, there will be an aggregate of 21 million bitcoins around and that is it- - positively no more will at any point be made. Given the current conversion scale, there are more than $1.4 billion bitcoins on the lookout.

The way bitcoin bargains work is fundamental, everybody has a bitcoin wallet that they use to send and acquire reserves. This wallet is a straightforward series of letters and numbers, helping make that wallet completely classified except if the person decides to interface themselves with it. The private substance of bitcoin bargains has made it be utilized for an assortment of illegal exercises. While disallowed buys may occur, there are a huge number of foundations, projects, and economies everywhere in the world that perceive bitcoin.

Bitcoin was at first planned by Satoshi Nakamoto in 2008 and the first bitcoin exchange occurred in 2009. If you had put resources into only a couple hundred US dollars in Bitcoin when it initially started, it would be esteemed at millions nowadays. Precisely the thing is you sitting tight for - go get your Bitcoins.

Coinbase and Bitcoin Startup

Coinbase, one of the world's biggest digital currency trades, was in the perfect spot at the perfect chance to gain by the spike in interest. To remain ahead in a lot bigger digital currency market, the organization is furrowing currency once again into its all-inclusive strategy. Coinbase, a San Francisco-based organization, is known as the main digital currency exchanging stage in the United States and with its proceeded progress, arrived at the No. 10 spots on the CNBC Disruptor list in 2018 after neglecting to make the rundown the past two years. On their way to progress, Coinbase has investigated every possibility of poaching key leaders from the New York Stock Exchange, Twitter, Facebook, and LinkedIn. In the current year, the size of its full-time designing group has practically multiplied.

Earn.com platform permits the clients to send and get advanced money while answering mass-market messages and finishing microtasks. Presently, the organization is wanting to bring a previous Andreessen Horowitz investor, earns originator, and CEO as its first-historically speaking boss technology official.

As indicated by the current valuation, Coinbase esteemed itself at about $8 billion when it set off to purchase Earn.Com. This worth is a lot higher than the valuation of $1.6 billion which was assessed at the last round of funding financing in the mid-year of 2017. Coinbase decays to remark on its valuation regardless of the way that it has more than $225 million in financing from top VC's including Union Square Ventures, Andreessen Horowitz, and the New York Stock Exchange.

To address the issues of institutional financial backers, the New York Stock Exchange is wanting to begin its digital money trade. Nasdaq, an opponent of NYSE is also considering a comparable move.

Contest is Coming

As contending associations hope to whittle down Coinbase's business, Coinbase is looking to other funding open doors trying to construct a channel around the organization. Dan Dolev, a Nomura moment investigator, said that Square, an organization run by Twitter CEO Jack Dorsey could eat into Coinbase's trade business since it began exchanging cryptographic money on its Square Currency application in January.

As indicated by the evaluations by Dolev, Coinbase's normal exchanging charges were generally 1.8 percent in 2017. Expenses this high could drive the clients to other less expensive trades. Coinbase is hoping to turn into an all-in-one resource for institutional financial backers while supporting its trade business. To bait in that white glove financial backer class, the organization reported an armada of new items. This class of financial backers has been particularly mindful to jump into the unpredictable cryptographic money market.

Coinbase Prime, The Coinbase Institutional Coverage Group, Coinbase Custody, and Coinbase Markets are the items dispatched by the organization. Coinbase feels that there are billions of dollars in an institutional currency that can be put resources into digital money. It as of now has the authority of $9 billion in client resources. Institutional financial backers are worried about security despite realizing Coinbase has never endured a hack like some other worldwide cryptographic money trades. Coinbase president and COO said that the catalyst of dispatching the Coinbase care last November was the absence of confided in overseers to defend their crypto resources.

Administrative Security Remains Intense

To keep access restricted to four cryptographic forms of money, Coinbase has drawn a great deal of analysis. However, they should proceed cautiously while the U.S. controllers purposeful on the most proficient method to police certain employments of the technology. For digital currency trades like Coinbase, the question of concern is whether cryptographic forms of money are protections that would be dependent upon the Securities and Exchange Commission locale. Coinbase is delayed to add new coins because the SEC declared in March that it would apply security laws to all digital money trades.

Wall Street Changes from Bashing Bit to Cryptocurrency Backer - How

As per the most recent information accessible from Autonomous Next Wall Street, interest in cryptographic money is by all accounts expanding. As of now, there are 287 crypto flexible investments, while in 2016, there were just 20 digital currency mutual funds that existed. Goldman Sachs has even opened a digital currency exchanging work area. Coinbase has likewise presented Coinbase Ventures, which is a hatchery reserve for beginning phase new businesses working in the digital currency and blockchain space. Coinbase Ventures has effectively collected $15 billion for additional speculations. Its first speculation was declared in a startup called Compound which permits one to acquire or loan cryptographic money while procuring a financing cost.

Toward the start of 2018, the organization dispatched Coinbase Commerce, which permits traders to acknowledge significant cryptographic forms of money for installment. Another bitcoin startup was BitPlay, which as of late collected $40 million in adventure currency. A year ago BitPlay prepared more than $1 billion in bitcoin installments. The defenders of blockchain technology accept that later on, cryptographic money will want to dispense with the requirement for focal financial specialists. All the while, it will bring down costs and make a decentralized monetary arrangement.

Why Use Bitcoin?

Bitcoin is nothing to joke about this moment, yet not every person gets why. All the more significantly, not every person gets whether Bitcoin is for them, and how they can get included. Here are few reasons why to Bitcoin.

Safer than banks

The absolute best programmers and online security specialists have made a pass at it, thus far nobody can discover any shortcomings. The Bitcoin Code has been portrayed as breathtakingly composed, the advanced identical to Shakespeare. Banking exchanges, in the meantime, are under a lower level of safety than Bitcoin. From multiple points of view, Bitcoin has must be safer than the banks. Although, the banks have been around for quite a long time, and people see how it works. However, Bitcoin is the new, youthful upstart, and necessities to substantiate itself.

Lower administration expenses than banks

Banking organizations charge high rates per exchange. The framework is set up such that person exchanges between two people are unthinkable; they require a "trusted" outsider to work with the exchange. What's more, normally, the banks will take a help charge for working with these exchanges. You can utilize escrow administrations with Bitcoin which takes an assistance charge, however, you don't need to. Since Bitcoin depends on P2P exchanges, there are no help charges. Normally, the banks are not a major devotee of Bitcoin also.

Okay of breakdown

When your currency is connected to an administration, it relies upon the soundness of that administration. Investigate the bills in your wallet. You buckled down for them.

Okay of swelling

The Bitcoins quantity is set at a foreordained rate. This means there is no chance of any administration printing off more currency to take care of their obligations. Though true monetary forms lose a little level of their value each year, the cost of Bitcoin is by all accounts getting consistently higher.

Since Bitcoin isn't joined to any administration or focal position, it doesn't rely upon any external conditions for its worth. Insofar as the web exists, Bitcoin will proceed to exist and be important.

The Far-Reaching Implications of the Bitcoin Protocol

It is difficult to envision a reality where cell phone technology is pervasive, and there are still people who don't approach sufficient monetary organizations. In these cutting-edge times, there are around six billion people with restricted or no admittance to banking offices. Hard to comprehend, isn't that so?

Unfortunately, this is a reality for some people in non-industrial nations. Combined with defilement, restricted methods of transportation, and high exchange charges, financial balances are an extravagance that numerous people can't manage. Enter Bitcoin into this condition and independence from the rat race is only the start.

Bitcoin isn't only currency for the web; it is a programming language that takes into consideration the decentralization of any data framework. As said by Andreas Antonopoulos (2014), "Bitcoin is the web of currency." In request to comprehend this present how about we utilize the similarity of the web; which permits any person admission to a worldwide correspondence and data network quickly.

In this equivalent manner, Bitcoin is permitting people moment admittance to a free worldwide monetary organization. The ramifications of a decentralized monetary organization liberated from the debasement of outsider arbitrators are overpowering. Consider briefly acquainting 6 billion expected purchasers with the worldwide commercial center. The opportunities for financial development and advancement are outstanding.

This exists because Satoshi Nakamoto, the designer of Bitcoin, decided to make open-source programming that gave all clients equivalent say. The force of the Bitcoin network is its clients, which as of now surpasses the consolidated processing force of the main 600 supercomputers on Earth.

This likens to an organization, which is for all goals of purposes, impervious. Every person PC goes about as a democratic hub. All together for the blockchain to be confirmed, a lion's share of the democratic hubs should validate if the condition is done accurately. This cycle occurs in nanoseconds, which means not all democratic hubs will partake in each given blockchain confirmation.

Bitcoin is fundamentally considered in the west as popular, new technology and a method for building riches. As of late, the notoriety of cryptographic forms of money has developed quickly inside venture circles, speculative stock investments, and among the innovatively disposed of because of its rising worth.

Although Bitcoin is used overwhelmingly inside these previously mentioned gatherings, the current buzz encompassing Bitcoin tycoons and the formal conferences in New York in regards to future guidelines have slung the currency into the standard (NPR). Nonetheless, restricting the Bitcoin convention to these recently referenced enterprises is very foolish given the virtuoso of Satoshi's hidden objective.

Keep in mind, the Bitcoin convention can be applied to any data framework, like the arrangement of casting a ballot. When applied to casting a ballot, there could be not, at this point the requirement for an outsider association to confirm a political decision as this is finished by every person democratic hub. This disposes of citizen extortion and casting a ballot machine altering. People would have the option to cast a ballot from the solaces of their own homes, utilizing evident ID codes, through a straightforward democratic framework.

We have seen that the Bitcoin convention not just has the ability to shape the fate of our worldwide monetary organization, however of our democracy, our telephones, and our digital TV. Any framework that depends on a fair-minded outsider arbiter can be supplanted by executing the Bitcoin programming. As the product is policed by all taking an interested person, the chance of defilement, or hacking the framework is minute.

Whether or not Bitcoin the currency at any point blooms into a genuine standard type of money-related exchange stays not yet clear, notwithstanding, the unrest in programming that Nakamoto has released has just barely started.

Simple 3-Step Guide to Buying Your First Bitcoin

Searching for a Bitcoin Buying Guide? Pondering where to begin? People have a ton of confusion about bitcoin - the absolute first generally known and acknowledged cryptographic money around the world. Many people think for instance that solitary programmers and obscure people use it. However, bitcoin is going standard with everybody from

TigerDirect to Expedia.com to Dell and even Subway tolerating installments in bitcoin now.

Why so popular?

Although, bitcoin has a lot of advantages over different monetary forms. For instance, you can send bitcoins to somebody as installment without going through the bank mediator (and get hit with additional expenses). It's likewise a lot quicker than sending currency through a bank wire or move.

With the entirety of this current, it's nothing unexpected that numerous people are presently attempting to purchase bitcoin interestingly. In any case, it's not as simple as going to your bank and pulling out bitcoins - or going to a store and plunking down some well-deserved money for bitcoin. The framework works a piece uniquely in contrast to that. This Bitcoin Buying Guide will go over a couple of things you need to know before you purchase - so you can purchase securely and safely.

Above all else, while the cost may be more than $2000 us per coin, you don't need to purchase a whole bitcoin. Most places will allow you to purchase bits of a bitcoin for just $20. So you can get going little and go from that point as you get more familiar with how things work. Besides, this article is for general purposes just and not to be taken as a monetary exhortation. Bitcoin can be unsafe and before making any buy, you ought to talk with your monetary consultant to check whether it's appropriate for you.

So here are 3 simple strides to purchasing Bitcoins:

Get a Bitcoin Wallet

The primary thing to do before you purchase your coins is to get a virtual wallet to store your coins. There are various sorts of wallets including ones you download to your telephone or PC, online wallets, and even offline cold stockpiling wallets.

Well-known wallets incorporate Blockchain, Armory, Bitgo Mycelium, and Xapo. Typically, it's pretty much as basic as downloading the wallet to your telephone as an application or downloading the product to your PC from the wallet's principal site.

Choose Where to Buy

Some online merchants will sell you bitcoins straightforwardly for money (or bank wire or charge card). There are also neighborhood trades that interface you up with merchants in your space hoping to sell. There are likewise ATMs where you go to buy with currency and get your coins conveyed to your wallet in minutes. Each bitcoin vendor has its advantages and downsides.

For instance, ATMs are incredible for security, yet they'll energize you to 20% on top of the current value, which is strange. (On a BTC cost of $2000, that $400! So you're paying $2400 rather than $2000). Regardless of where you choose to purchase, make sure to do your exploration and go with a believed merchant with a decent standing and solid client support. First-time purchasers will particularly have questions and may require additional help to assist them with their first exchange.

Odds of Using Bitcoins for Illegal Activities

Bitcoin intermediaries are progressively turning into a significant element in bitcoin exchanging. They ensure brokers get an incentive for their currency. Although, they are legitimate in many nations throughout the planet albeit a few wards seriously confine unfamiliar monetary forms while different locales limit the permitting of such trades. Controllers drawn from different locales are cautiously finding a way ways to offer the two people and organizations rules and guidelines on the best way to approach coordinating the framework with the formal and directed monetary framework.

Bitcoins are currency, and currency is frequently used to work with both lawful and illicit exchanges. However, currency, the current financial framework, and MasterCard have outperformed the framework to fund wrongdoing. Accordingly, the advantages of these developments are considered a long way past the expected downsides. The framework has been planned so that brings in currency safer. Also, the framework can go about as significant security against any type of monetary wrongdoing.

Besides, the framework is difficult to fake. Also, clients are in all-out control of the installments and can't acquire unapproved accuses as it occurs of MasterCard extortion. The exchanges of this framework are irreversible and insusceptible to fake chargebacks. The framework makes it feasible for currency to be appropriately gotten against misfortune and robbery utilizing helpful and solid components like reinforcements, various marks, and encryption.

Bitcoins and taxes

The framework isn't viewed as fiat money that has accomplished a legitimate delicate status inside any ward. Although, charge responsibility frequently gathers paying little heed to the medium utilized. An assortment of enactment exists in various locales which causes deals, pay, capital additions, finance, or some other sort of responsibility to get a show with this currency exchanging stage.

Guideline of the framework

The convention can't be altered without the collaboration of every one of its clients who select the kind of programming to utilize. Any endeavors to dole out rights to the nearby position when you consider the standards of the organization are impractical. A rich association can select to put essentially in mining to control a large portion of the processing influence of the framework. This would get the association to a position where it can converse or hinder ongoing exchanges. By the by, the association has no assurance that it could keep a similar force since it would need to contribute more than the wide range of various excavators throughout the planet.

5 Tips to Consider Before Investing in Bitcoin

In 2017, Bitcoin encountered a ton of development and people raked in tons of currency all the while. Indeed, even today, Bitcoin is quite possibly the most worthwhile business sector. If you are only now getting started, you might need to get your work done before placing currency in Bitcoin. Given beneath are 5 master tips that can assist you with keeping away from basic errors while you exchange Bitcoins.

Become familiar with the Basics First

Most importantly, you might need to get familiar with the rudiments so you can find out about how to purchase and sell Bitcoin. In addition, you might need to peruse audits of mainstream Bitcoin trades to search for the best stage. Likewise, with different sorts of monetary ventures, you might need to discover approaches to secure your speculation. Ensure that your resources are protected against con artists and digital assaults. Although, security is the main part of a venture.

Set Clear Targets

Since Bitcoin is another market, you may think that it's difficult to realize the opportune chance to exchange your Bitcoin. You might not have any desire to settle on the slip-up of settling on venture choices dependent on your feelings. Taking shrewd actions can assist you with limiting misfortunes and gain great headway.

Put resources into Bitcoin

The Bitcoin mining industry is ascending in fame at a high speed. Afterward, it was feasible to mine Bitcoin in unique server farms as it were. Today, if you need to construct a locally established mining community, you may need to burn through millions. Also, it's smarter to put resources into Bitcoins.

Consider the Market Cap

The digital currency esteem is substantial just if you think about the current inventory available for use. If you need to buy Bitcoin, don't zero in a lot on the current worth of the currency. Although, you might need to consider the total market cap.

Enhance your Investments

New Bitcoin financial backers will in general have brief energy for cryptographic money. Indeed, With Bitcoin, you can enhance your venture hazard. If you put resources into digital money shrewdly, you can appreciate the very rewards that you do by putting resources into Forex. You might not have any desire to place every one of your eggs in a similar bin. Thus, you might need to put resources into other digital currencies too.

Shrewd Bitcoin Strategies to Accumulate Gold Bullion

Discover an organization that sells gold bullion

There are numerous online organizations online that sell gold bullion, yet there are not very many that offer motivation programs once you become their customer. The organization needs to offer quality items, like selling gold bullion in little sizes of 1 gram, 2.5 gram, and 5 grams. The motivating force programs need to permit you to acquire commissions once you allude people to the organization.

Begin mining bitcoin online or offline

There are two fundamental approaches to get bitcoin. Mine bitcoin online or offline. To mine bitcoin online is simple and a lot less difficult than offline techniques. You should be mindful of this alternative also because a great many tricksters are professing to have a bitcoin ranch, however, indeed, don't. There are also trusted and genuine organizations that have bitcoin ranches working every day that I for one use. You can likewise mine bitcoin offline by buying a bitcoin digger, which is PC equipment that you set up at your home. This bitcoin will then naturally be shipped off your online bitcoin wallet.

Open an online bitcoin wallet

You will require a spot to store your bitcoin once you are prepared to begin inside the digital money market. Search for an organization that offers a wallet to store bitcoin and an offline vault to secure it. Numerous programmers are attempting to break into the wallets of online clients and take all their bitcoin. If you store your bitcoin offline, you won't ever be a casualty of online programmers.

Buy gold bullion with bitcoin

Since you have bitcoin coming in consistently there are quite certain ways that should be followed to buy gold bullion from the organization you picked. You need to connect your bitcoin wallet to a visa card.

What Makes Bitcoin Different?

So what makes Bitcoin unique about every one of a great many different coins which have been concocted since?

When Bitcoin was first developed it started to spread gradually among a little gathering of people. It developed naturally. When people began to see the advantages of Bitcoin and how the cost would increment because of its fixed stock, it started to become quicker. The Bitcoin blockchain is currently spread across a huge number of PCs everywhere in the world. It has spread outside the ability to control any administration. Its maker has disappeared and now it runs self-sufficiently.

Engineers can redesign and improve the Bitcoin network however this must be finished by agreement all through the entire Bitcoin organization. No single person can handle Bitcoin. This is the thing that makes Bitcoin remarkable and difficult to imitate. There are a large number of other digital currencies accessible now however to act as an illustration of what makes Bitcoin unique, I'll use Ethereum for instance. It's one of the greatest Altcoins at this moment and has been since it was designed in 2015 by Vitalik Buterin. Vitalik controls the Ethereum blockchain and essentially has the last say on any improvement that occurs on Ethereum.

Everybody should possess some Bitcoin. It's not without it's risky, however. If you're new to Bitcoin, you ought to learn however much you can before you put away any currency. Possessing Bitcoin accompanies a great deal of obligation. Figure out how to utilize Bitcoin securely. For people simply entering the universe of cryptographic forms of money, there are bunches of covered-up threats.

The purchasing and selling measure costs currency, which is the motivation that trades need to run as organizations. However, not at all like with the purchasing of stocks or bonds, these trades normally charge a rate. This interaction is not quite the same as rebate financiers that most financial backers utilize that typically charge expenses dependent on a level rate. This implies that over the long run, purchasing and selling can get very expensive. It is a smart thought to converse with bitcoin dealers about the most ideal choices before you start.

A host tracker is an instrument that can gauge the openness of a site. Consider the various contemplations and consider your exceptional conditions with the goal that you can pick the best trade for you. Luckily, numerous online assets make it simple to complete exploration and you can get all the data that you need.

Conclusion:

Bitcoin has been known by numerous people to be the most renowned decentralized digital money. In any case, other than bitcoin, there exist other altcoins that present an incredible worth too. Bitcoin money is an analysis that has attempted the decentralized organization convention execution. Until now, Bitcoin has been fruitful in numerous spaces that the current brought together monetary systems have fizzled. In the monetary area, which is intricate and requesting, Bitcoin has shown that it's ready to deal with numerous other genuine issues we face on the Internet today.

Utilizing Bitcoin as a decentralized improvement stage inside the Linux bit would take into account a simpler safer, solid, decentralized execution of the most famous Internet conventions being used today. Conventions could be joined into the core of working systems utilizing decentralized technology.

This methodology would deliver Internet users from reliance on outsiders to get to services like SMTP, VOIP, DNS, and other Internet-based services. Subsequently, the Internet-based services would be decentralized, more affordable to oversee, and their service approaches more available to user impact.